A souvenir guide

Brean Down
Somerset

Nick Hanks

G000299796

Brean Down Through History	2
Sands of time	4
Rock of ages	6
A place of prayer	8
Defending the down	10
A half-built harbour	12
A new attraction	14
At war once more	16
Training the troops	18
A new line of defence	20
Flora and Fauna of the Down	22
On and around the down	24
Almost an Island	26
The importance of Brean Down	28
A changing environment	30
A 360° tour	32

National Trust

Brean Down Through History

Brean Down reaches out into the surging tidal waters of the Severn Estuary, affording stunning views across Somerset, Exmoor and South Wales. It has a long, rich history and, unusually, has visible features for all periods right back to the last Ice Age.

Brean Down is the tip of the Mendips, cut off by the River Axe. Within its 1.2-mile (2-kilometre) length are remains stretching from the Second World War to the last Ice Age. Uniquely, this peninsula contains sands of international importance, sands that have accumulated since the last Ice Age, a period of about 70,000 years. A study of this unusual accumulation reveals changes in climate and clues about the way people lived through all that time. Brean Down's national and international importance is recognised by its designation as a Site of Special Scientific Interest (SSSI), a Scheduled Ancient Monument (SAM) and a Special Area of Conservation.

Above Enjoying far-reaching views today, Brean Down has been millennia in the making

Past lives

There is a treasure trove of archaeological remains: Bronze Age settlements, burial mounds and fields; a Roman temple demolished to build a very early Christian hermitage, as well as a Romano-British cemetery; an Iron Age hillfort that survived the Roman invasion of AD 43; an abandoned port; a Victorian coastal fort built to fend off invasion but destroyed in a huge explosion, and then refortified in the Second World War. There are odd-looking structures used for secret-weapon testing and military training exercises. Additionally, there are the remains of the homes of the people who lived here, including soldiers, workers and their families.

Present attractions

Brean Down is as rich in ecology as it is in archaeology. There is a community of plants on the down's southern slope that grows nowhere else. Remarkably, it has been here since the end of the last Ice Age. The down creates a rich patchwork of habitats, supporting a wide variety of flowers, shrubs, birds and butterflies. The surrounding estuary is also home to many wading birds.

Any of these things are rare in themselves, but together they make Brean Down exceptional. It is hardly surprising that this is such an inspiring place, valued for both study and recreation, visited and enjoyed by thousands each year.

Sands of time

Up against the cliffs on the south side of the down, sand has been continuously accumulating for the last 70,000 years. Most visitors walk right over this without giving it a second thought, unaware of its uniqueness.

These sands of time, when studied by scientists, reveal clues about the way the climate has changed over millennia, in particular the fluctuations at the end of the last Ice Age about 11,500 years ago. This wedge of sandy material forms the join between the down and the surrounding fields. In its exposed end, known as the sand cliff, actual Ice Age period features can be seen.

An Ice Age menagerie

Archaeological examination of the exposed cliff face and its upper surface has revealed a rich and complex history. The lowest levels accumulated during the last 60,000 years of the last Ice Age and contain the bones of many creatures that once lived here including: field vole, owl, duck, snow lemming, Hensel's lemming, arctic fox, arctic hare, horse, reindeer, giant deer, bison, wolf and even mammoth.

The main bulk of the sand in the cliff was swept up against the down as the result of some unknown but massive change in the landscape around 20,000 years ago. Above and below this sand are alternating layers of more and less angular stone fragments fractured out of the cliff by ice. These indicate the varying intensities of temperature. Originally these deposits would have stretched along the length of the down's southern cliffs, but much of the sand cliff has been eroded. It is still vulnerable to erosion today as it is mostly soft sand.

Other Ice Age soils survive in a cave on the beach called 'Reindeer Rift'. This is part of a cave system that runs under the down, but which is blocked by red earth from the last Ice Age and some animal bone. At this time the sea level was much lower, and the River Severn was in a gorge far away between the islands of Steep Holm and Flat Holm, which were then hills.

Above The sands of the south side of the down, to the right of the image, have accumulated over thousands of years

Home for so many, for so long

In the upper section of these sands are even more complex layers. These extend back from the sand cliff under all the routes that lead onto the down. The changing climate and vegetation after the thaw at the end of the Ice Age enabled a new agricultural use of the down. There is a sequence of Bronze Age settlements with roundhouses, which left evidence of weaving, jewellery, pottery and flint tools. The inhabitants had domesticated animals (cattle, sheep, pigs, goats, horse and dogs) and grew crops (wheat, barley, emmer and spelt). However, they also fished, foraged and hunted, as their ancestors did before them. Brean Down is one of the earliest sites with evidence of salt production in Europe, then a valuable commodity for trading. The settlements would have been more extensive but most of the site has been lost to the sea.

Onwards and upwards

As the rising sea finally reached its current level, the people of Brean seem to have moved up onto the down, where they later built a hillfort (300 to 100 BC). They may have moved there to be closer to the River Axe, which passes right by the east end of the down. The hillfort was occupied through the Roman period (AD 43 to 410), when the surrounding levels were drained for farming.

In the 5th to early 7th centuries, the post-Roman dwellers on the down buried their dead in stone-lined graves aligned west–east in the sand cliff area. This was probably an early Christian cemetery, suggested by the presence of the 'hermit's hut' built above by the site of the demolished Roman temple (see pages 8–9). After this period, the people decamped to establish the nearby settlement of Brean village and farm the drained levels.

Right The cave known as 'Reindeer Rift'

Rock of ages

Brean Down has been occupied, almost continuously, for thousands of years. As we've seen, evidence of people's everyday lives was buried in the layers of the down, but they also left their marks on its surface.

The wind that continuously sweeps over the down would have kept it partly free of the woodland that colonised the lower-lying land after the ice receded. So this hill would have attracted early farmers in the Neolithic era (early Stone Age, 4000–2,500 BC) to make their fields here. The banks that were once field boundaries stretch the length of the level ground across the top of the down. The best surviving ones can be clearly seen across the West Knoll. Amongst these are Bronze Age burial mounds of various sizes, in which were interred the cremated bones of the dead.

Mystery mound

Between the top of the concrete steps and a natural rock ridge, there is a low mound, 40 feet (12 metres) in length, aligned west–east and made mostly of stones. It is wider at the east end (20 feet, 6 metres) than it is at the west end (10 feet, 3 metres). There is also the faint trace of a ditch on the south side, but a former footpath has disturbed the north side. This shape and location is typical of Neolithic long barrows, which were used for ritual and burial. A few shards of Neolithic pottery and flint have been found nearby to support this theory; however, this would make it the smallest known example of a long barrow of this period.

Early fortifications

In the Iron Age a small hillfort was built here, enclosing the east end of the down in a ditch and bank. The builders incorporated the cliffs in the design, and so only needed to build an earthwork across the level ground along the west side, where the Military Road now passes. A small excavation across the south-west section of ditch and bank in 1974 revealed that there had been a wall, 8 feet (2.5 metres) wide, with a walkway running behind it on top of the bank, built between 300–100 BC. Over 680 limpet shells were found, which had been discarded in the ditch shortly after it was dug. This may have been part of a celebratory feast on the completion of the work. Inside the hillfort there would have been roundhouses, and a few of these survived to be recorded in the 19th century. A little pottery and other finds show that the hillfort remained in use during the Roman period. However, the most significant activity at this time was the construction of a temple on the East Knoll that faced inland towards Glastonbury.

Medieval modifications

During the Middle Ages, the period of time from the 5th to the 15th centuries, areas of the East Knoll were ploughed, creating fields and leaving the corrugated undulations known as ridge and furrow. Part of the down was also used to raise rabbits, a rare and valuable meat at that time, in artificial warrens known as pillow mounds. A cottage was built for the keeper of the warren, known as a warrener, on top of the sand cliff. Salt production started again nearby and Brean Down Farm was built. The rearing of rabbits ended around 1600. The warrener's cottage was abandoned and left as it was, leaving complete pottery vessels for later archaeologists to discover, a rare find among the fragments they normally uncover.

Tsunami on the Severn

On 20 January 1607, the whole of the Severn Estuary was affected by a great flood as far inland as Glastonbury. It was probably a tsunami. The wave was 'affirmed to have runne …. with a swiftness so incredible as that no gray-hounde could have escaped' and described as 'mighty hilles of water tumbling over one another in such a sort as if the greatest mountains in the world had overwhelmed the lowe villages'. It is estimated to have been 5.5 metres (18 feet) high and moved at 32 mph (51 kph). John Good of Brean lost his wife, five children and nine servants. He survived by clinging on to some thatch, which carried him for over a mile.

Opposite Winds keep this exposed headland relatively clear of woodland, an attraction for early farmers

A place of prayer

For millennia people have been attracted to Brean Down, as a safe, elevated settlement, easy to defend, where they could forage, fish and farm to feed their families, but also for its uplifting views – a place for contemplation.

Around AD 340 a Roman temple was built on the East Knoll, the site being ideal: on a prominent hilltop and beside an earlier sacred site – the, by then, ancient round barrow known as 'the Potter's Mound'. The location would suggest that the temple may have been dedicated to the goddess of the River Severn.

It was used for rituals, indicated by the Roman pottery found in the upper layers of the mound when local antiquarian Reverend J. Skinner investigated it in 1819. In the 1980s a small, thin sheet of lead folded in three was found on the beach below. On it was an inscription almost too worn to be read. Analysis revealed that the inscription was a Roman 'curse' addressed to a goddess, but the name could not be read. These lead curses are requests to a deity for help, written in the style of a contract.

The temple was expanded before 367, with the addition of a porch with Tuscan columns, and two small annexes, possibly intended as accommodation for a resident priest or priestess. However, an excavation in 1958 revealed that the temple seemed to have been little used. The finds can be seen on display at Weston-Super-Mare Museum, and with care some of the outline of the temple can still be traced on the ground.

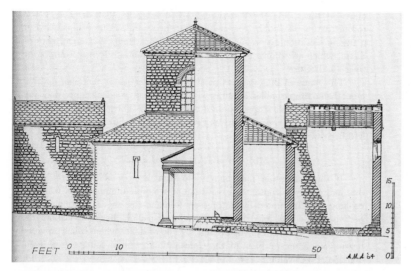

Left The view from the site of the Roman temple overlooking the River Severn

Top A reconstruction of Brean Down's temple

Above The outline of the Roman temple, completely excavated and photographed in the 1950s

FEET 0 10 50

Worship repurposed

A Roman temple is a fascinating discovery in itself; however, what makes this temple particularly interesting is what happened after its 30 years of use. It became semi-derelict and then people moved into it. They cooked in it, used part of the building for metal-working, and amongst the items they left behind was a playing piece from some kind of board game. Then the building was thoroughly ransacked, with holes dug in the floors and plaster hacked off the walls. They were presumably looking for treasure, but all they found were a few low-denomination coins, which they threw in to the rubble.

Finally, the whole building was systematically dismantled. All of the walls' plaster was chipped off the stones before they were taken away for some unknown use. Then, around 390, something very curious occurred. A new building was built from the stone of the temple and one of the doors was possibly also reclaimed. However, the temple's foundations were not re-used, despite this new building being the same size as one of the annexes. For reasons unknown, it was built on a different orientation to the original temple, between the site of the temple and the Potter's Mound. This building was occupied by one individual, who slept and cooked food in a single room, 10 feet (3 metres) by 8 feet (2.5 metres). The occupant lived here for many years collecting shellfish, keeping pigs and sheep. They also spun wool, possibly to make their own clothing. This occupant may have been the skeleton buried nearby in the rubble of the site of the temple, before this hut was also demolished.

But who would live in such a modest way in such a windswept spot? No other dwelling on the down was so exposed. A possibility is that it may have been the home of an early Christian hermit of the generation of St Patrick. This suggestion is made more likely as there is an early Christian cemetery dating to between the 400s and the 600s on the sand cliff below.

Defending the down

In the mid-19th century a fort was constructed here as one of a series built along the south coast as a defence against the French. Britain and France weren't at war, but tensions were high over territory disputes in Europe and Africa. However, these defensive measures ultimately backfired at Brean Down.

At the time Brean Down was part of the Wyndham estate, the farm and some of the surrounding land having been bought by Sir Wadham Wyndham in 1663. The family retained ownership into the 20th century, but were not directly involved in managing the land, preferring to lease it to local farmers. It wasn't until the mid-19th century that Brean Down was pressed into more active service.

Palmerston's plans

Lord Palmerston was First Lord of the Treasury in 1861, when a French intervention in Italy caused an invasion scare. He responded by setting up The Royal Commission on the Defence of the United Kingdom, the most ambitious and expensive defence building programme that the UK had ever contemplated, with dozens of forts built along the south coast.

Brean Down Fort is one of five Palmerston forts built to guard the Bristol Channel. The others were located on Flat Holm and Steep Holm, the two islands you can see in the channel, and across the water in Wales, in Penarth and Barry Island. These were smaller fortifications, known as batteries, which are emplacements for heavy guns.

Above The window of the Master Gunner's quarters

Right The high walls and deep defensive moat of the fort

Opposite top The fort occupying its position at the tip of the down

Opposite below A plan of the Victorian fort's gun emplacements before they were covered by new gun positions in the Second World War

Building a defence

The fort at the west end of Brean Down was built 1865–72. The Military Road was built along the down, avoiding the main slopes. This is the route most visitors follow to the fort. If the harbour had been finished (see over), there would have been a railway line running along the down below the road.

The guns faced out to sea to defend the River Severn from enemy shipping. The landward side was defended by gun slits and a deep dry moat cut into the rock. This Victorian phase of the fort is built from limestone quarried nearby. The main building was the barracks for 50 men. The smaller building was for the Master Gunner and his family. The gun positions were for four seven-inch RMLs (Rifle Muzzle Loaded) guns mounted on 'A' pivots (rotated at the muzzle)

and three mounted on 'C' pivots (rotated in the middle). The best surviving example is 'Gun No.1', which still has the pivot, made from an old cannon, and 'Gun No.2'. There are large magazines below ground, where the cartridges and shells were stored separately for safety.

This was proved to be a sound measure, for at 5am on 6 July 1900 Gunner Haines fired his rifle into 'No.3 Magazine' through a vent, exploding nearly three tons of ammunition. He was killed and a few others sustained minor injuries; the inquest concluded that it was suicide. Half of the fort was damaged or destroyed, and melted zinc debris from cartridge cases was scattered all over the down. The extent of the damage can be traced, as the areas where the limestone Victorian structures are missing have since been covered by concrete.

A half-built harbour

Brean Down has long been valued as a prime site for defence. However, when not at war, or perhaps to pay for wars, people have always needed to trade with other countries. The down's location made the establishment of a harbour here an attractive, but challenging, proposition.

From the 1840s there had been talk of a harbour being built at Brean to provide safe anchorage for Royal Mail Ships, and to act as a port for crossing the Atlantic, as it has a slight advantage in terms of distance over Liverpool.

The Brean Down Harbour Company was formed in 1861 with a capital of £350,000. The Bristol and Exeter Railway entered into an agreement to provide a link with the main railway network from a line extending the whole length of the down. The project began in November 1864 with a celebration of the laying of the foundation stone. Over 200 local dignitaries, company officials and the town band sailed from Weston-Super-Mare in *The Wye*, a paddle steamer, to see Lady Eardley Wilmot lower the foundation stone amid speeches, champagne and general celebration. However, at the crucial moment not all of the buoyancy aids came free, so the stone sank, but not completely. The tide took it all the way to Steep Holm.

Below The Brean Down Harbour project, imagined in 1864

This was a poor start and things did not improve. The construction workers were here for four years, but the project was beset with difficulties: the main contractor died, the company leaders argued and heavy storms destroyed much of the early construction. In 1868 the contractor on the fort, John Perry, stopped the work because he was disgusted by the frequent changes of plan: 'the constant building up and pulling down', apparently due to 'the extraordinary views of the government representative'. A line of shaped blocks and a few stone bollards are all that remains.

A quarry on Brean Down supplied the stone for both the fort and the never-completed harbour. Around the quarry there are the slight remains of houses built for the two teams of workers. This is a rare survival for such temporary structures. There would have been countless such dwellings for the itinerant workers across Britain who built the railways, canals and infrastructure of the Industrial Revolution (1820–40). Their families lived here too, and at least one child Alice Boley, was born here. Thomas Stevens, the owner of Brean Down Farm, set up the Brean Down Mission and read to the children because there was no school.

Left A section of the harbour wall

Below Bollards from the abandoned harbour are strewn on the rocks below Brean Down

Entrepreneur or rogue?

One of the workers was a colourful character, Frederick Harris the boatman. He had run the pub on Steep Holm, where in 1857 a bear mauled a visitor. Rather than paying compensation, Frederick elected to give away all his assets and have a friend arrest him, thus getting himself declared penniless and homeless. Somehow, by the time construction work on the fort ended in 1872, this bankrupt boatman had become the owner of the Claremont Royal Pier Hotel in Weston-Super-Mare.

A new attraction

The rise of Weston-super-Mare as a tourist destination in the Victorian period (1837–1901) was inevitably going to affect Brean Down. This stand-out feature was clearly visible from the town's seafront and naturally drew the crowds.

Most visitors would have walked along the town's promenade and beach to Uphill, from where they would have taken the ferry (which closed in 1996) across the River Axe. Then they would have passed Brean Down Farm House Restaurant, which welcomed visitors with: 'Home Produce & Cold Luncheons & Teas. Refreshments. Closed Sundays.' For those who came along the road from Brean village there

was a small, thatched cottage with a flag proclaiming 'Beach Teas'.

From 1910–36 the fort was used as the Old Fort Picnic Refreshment Rooms, which was open in the summer months. The soldiers' barrack block became the café. In 1925, in the former Master Gunner's quarters, lived Alfred Meredith and his wife, who ran the café. They hired 22-year-old Irene Sampson to work for them as a waitress for 10s a week. She cycled the 6-mile (10-kilometre) round trip to Brean village every day to collect two cans of milk. Their water came from a well and there was a small vegetable garden beside the moat. A playground was constructed in the courtyard, and the entry charge to the fort was a penny.

Above Tourists making the crossing to Brean Down in 1918

Opposite top Mrs Jenkins feeding the chickens outside the Old Fort Picnic Refreshment Rooms; she lived at the fort in 1916

Opposite middle Captain Cox the Brean Down warden keeping watch in about 1943

Opposite bottom Captain Cox's New House

The down's last resident

In 1909, with visitor numbers continuing to grow, the Wyndham estate appointed a wildlife warden for Brean Down and Steep Holm. Captain Harry Cox of Weston got the job after retiring from service in the Indian Army, and remained in post until his death in 1949, making him the last resident on the down.

He was naturally very knowledgeable about the down and its wildlife. He was popular with the children and he would lend them his binoculars so they could watch the badgers in their sett. He also took young people, including Irene Sampson, on trips to the island in his leaky motorboat, which invariably required bailing out with a treacle tin on the way.

Captain Harry Cox had two homes on Brean Down. His 'Old House' was a tin hut, sheltered from the prevailing wind under the northern edge of the West Knoll about halfway along the Military Road. His water supply was a barrel that collected rain from the roof. Irene Sampson saw him filling his kettle with water from a barrel covered in green algae. She told him he shouldn't drink that and he replied: 'That won't kill me. Anyway I am going to boil it.'

'Cox's New House' was built between 1938 and 1941 nearer the Military Road and in the ditch of the hillfort. Much more substantial, it had two rooms built with re-used stone from the fort, including arched doorways. The roof is made of flat thin concrete. The main room has fine views of Weston Bay through large windows, and had a timber floor. The rear room has a solid floor and heavy iron shutters. This may possibly have been used for storage of military equipment used in the adjacent training area, with Captain Harry Cox to keep an eye on it.

At war once more

In the middle of the 20th century, Britain faced a new and very real threat of invasion, this time by German forces. The world was at war, declared in 1939, and the fort at Brean Down was pressed into service once more.

Above This two-storey building accommodated battle HQ above and battery command below

Right These cabinets were used to store the shells for the naval guns

Brean Down was re-fortified in 1941, and two large concrete gun emplacements were built to defend the estuary. Though new, they held second-hand guns that had formerly been on ships. Their range was 20 miles (32 kilometres), which is twice the width of the Bristol Channel at this point. The bolts that attached the guns to the concrete can still be seen, as can the lockers the shells were stored in. The Victorian barracks became the cookhouse and canteen. The Master Gunner's quarters became the officers' mess.

The soldiers and officers lived in Nissen hut barracks in the old quarry outside the fort. You can still see the huts' concrete bases. The longest base was a training room, where models were used to practise rangefinding. Beside the road are the bases for a vehicle-inspection pit and the fort's checkpoint.

Above these is the best-preserved World War II building on the complex, which is still roofed. Constructed on two levels, the only connection between them was a hole used for passing notes. The upper room was the battle headquarters for 571 Coast Regiment; the lower was the battery command for Brean Down, in which you can still see the pillar that supported the rangefinder, an instrument for estimating the distance of an object or target. It also contained the telephone exchange, and you can just trace the line of the phone cables down to where they emerge by the moat and the pillar of the Victorian rangefinder. These rangefinders were sited above the fort for a wide view and so that the smoke from the guns would not obscure their observations.

At the tip of the down, at the water's edge, are two buildings for searchlights. The World War II phase of the fort is an even rarer survival than that for the Victorian era.

Above A rare photo taken inside a battery command showing the rangefinder in use

Training the troops

While it never came under enemy fire, Brean Down made a significant contribution to the war effort as a training base. In addition to this, the fort was used for the covert development of weapons, with varying degrees of success.

Here the Department of Miscellaneous Weapons Development (DWMD) tested various devices of destruction. Amongst these was a variation on the bouncing bomb used in the famous Dam Busters raid of May 1943. It was called Project Baseball, and consisted of a sphere of explosives intended to be launched from boats. It was test-fired from the rails that can be seen below the fort pointing out towards Steep Holm. On the third test it reached 230 feet per second (70 metres per second) and exploded, severely damaging the rails.

Another secret weapon was called the Expendable Noise Maker. It was designed to attract enemy acoustic torpedoes. During testing it accidently misfired and destroyed a chicken coop, though the farmer inside survived.

Right The rails used for launching explosive spheres as part of Project Baseball

Target practice

Another rarity from this period is the group of World War II training structures in and around the hillfort end of the down. In the middle there is a large concrete arrow. Nearby, the square concrete slabs on brick pillars are what remains of the Range Control Bunker. The arrow guided aircraft for bombing practice to targets in Bridgwater Bay. However, sometimes the arrow itself was used as a target for bags of white chalk dropped instead of bombs, with the officers in the unglazed Range Control Bunker the 'accidental' targets.

Within the hillfort to the south of the road are the remains of two water tanks, and to the north, a flat area for fire-fighting training. Beyond this are six brick Lewis gun emplacements. You can see the metal bolts in the concrete that held them. This type of mounting could also have held photographic equipment, bomb aimers, navigation equipment or have been used for gun calibration.

On the beach below the high limestone cliffs are a couple of concrete platforms with rusting metal attachments. These were used on 3 June 1943 to demonstrate rockets that carried ladders and climbing ropes. These were then used by US Rangers on D-Day, 6 June 1944, to scale the cliffs on Pointe Du Hoc Battery, Normandy.

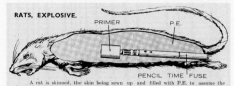

RATS, EXPLOSIVE.

PRIMER   P.E.

PENCIL TIME FUSE

A rat is skinned, the skin being sewn up and filled with P.E. to assume the shape of a dead rat. A Standard No. 6 Primer is set in the P.E. Initiation is by means of a short length of safety fuse with a No. 27 detonator crimped on one end, and a copper tube igniter on the other end, or, as in the case of the illustration above, a P.T.F. with a No. 27 detonator attached. The rat is then left amongst the coal beside a boiler and the flames initiate the safety fuze when the rat is thrown on to the fire, or as in the case of the P.T.F. a Time Delay is used.

Wartime wheezes

The Department of Miscellaneous Weapons Development (DMWD), known colloquially as the Wheezers and Dodgers, was responsible for the development of various unconventional weapons during World War II. The nickname was derived from their original title, the Inspectorate of Anti-Aircraft Weapons and Devices, which was corrupted to 'Instigator of Anti-Aircraft Wheezes and Dodges'. Among the more outlandish ideas were Bat Bombs (consisting of a bomb-shaped casing with over a thousand compartments, each containing a hibernating Mexican Free-tailed Bat with a small incendiary device attached), and rat carcasses filled with plastic explosives.

Above These platforms supported demonstrations of rocket-propelled ladders used in the D-Day landings

Below These structures were training gun positions

A new line of defence

During the 20th century Brean Down increasingly became valued for its wildlife and history, and defensive measures of a different kind were required.

It became protected by law as a Site of Special Scientific Interest (SSSI), a Scheduled Ancient Monument (SAM) and a Special Area of Conservation. Leased as an RSPB reserve from 1912 to 1952, it passed shortly after into the ownership of the National Trust. The Victorian fort was passed to the Trust from Sedgemoor District Council in 2002.

Research and excavations were carried out, which gradually increased the understanding of the down. The University of Bristol Speleological Society excavated the Roman temple in 1958, and the hillfort was excavated in 1974. English Heritage (now Historic England) excavated the sand cliff with its Bronze Age settlements between 1983–87.

Over-enthusiastic tidying

Management practices at Brean Down have changed greatly over the course of the 20th century. The fort and the World War II structures were at one time regarded as unimportant and untidy, with the unfortunate consequence that they were steadily tidied away by enthusiastic bands of students and the unemployed as part of the Manpower Services Commission, set up in the 1970s.

The plastic armour roof of the two fort gun emplacements was destroyed with high explosives by the 54 Squadron Junior Leaders Regiment. Also, an Iron Age roundhouse beside the Military Road was mistaken for a small gun emplacement, filled in and levelled.

A balancing act

The National Trust has installed props to support the roofs of some of the buildings and repeatedly removes the vegetation from other vulnerable structures such as the Nissen hut bases. However, many of the structures were only intended for temporary use, and so were not strongly built, such as the training gun emplacements in the hillfort. Also, those closest to the power of the sea can have little done to protect them. For example, the naval searchlight at the very end of the down has lost its access walkway and the building has had its roof flipped over by the sea (see photo on page 18).

Helping to control the invasive bracken and scrub that suppresses the wild flowers, a feral herd of goats grazes the more inaccessible areas of the down all year round. Sheep and cattle complement this with periodic grazing of the rest of the down. From time to time, to maintain the balance between the habitats, areas of the down require clearance of bracken by machine and the cutting of scrub by hand.

With sites such as Brean Down a fine balance has to be struck between preserving what visitors are coming to see, and providing access to see them. The thin soils of the down mean that if there are too many visitors, the soil will rapidly wear away, meaning the loss of plants and the animals that live on them as well as damage to archaeological remains. Some areas of thick vegetation need to be cleared for visitors and wild flowers, but many animals also require undisturbed areas to hide in. Consequently the condition of the down is regularly monitored.

Opposite An aerial view of Brean Down taken in the 1980s

Below A population of wild goats now keeps the bracken and scrub down

Flora and Fauna
of the Down

Brean Down boasts a variety of habitats in a relatively small area. There is a coast of mud flats, dunes and cliffs, which surround wind-clipped slopes, rich grassland and scrubby woodland.

A whole series of influences that vary across the down modify these habitats further: the aspect to wind and sun; slope and drainage; different animals' grazing habits; human footfall; exposure to sea spray; varying soil depth and composition. This richness is recognised by the down being designated a Site of Special Scientific Interest (SSSI) and a Special Area of Conservation.

The many faces of the down

The southern slope is particularly species-rich and the most important habitat on the down. Here, a unique plant community has survived undisturbed since the end of the last Ice Age. The strong prevailing winds have kept this part of the down free of trees and shrubs for over 10,000 years. Amazingly, this hillside would look familiar to the people of that time. The plants here are small and cling to the shallow soil. The white rock rose (see over) is a particular feature of the down's flora. It grows in abundance and is easy to find, but be very careful when approaching this steep slope.

Along the top of the down the thin, alkaline soil supports an outstandingly rich limestone grassland. These species blend with the rarer plants on the southern slope but create a

different character to the crest of the hills. The northern slopes are gentler and have deeper soils. Here the ridge of the down provides shelter from the wind, and the sand can settle and mingle with the soils, turning them more acidic. The soil is even more acidic on the ancient dune of the sand cliff.

The Severn Estuary around the down is also an SSSI. The vast mud flats are formed by silt carried by four major rivers: the Avon, Usk, Wye and Severn. Twice a day they are swept by a 48-foot (15-metre) tide, one of the highest tides in the world. These mud flats provide important feeding grounds for migrating and over-wintering waterfowl.

Brean's birds and beasts

This patchwork of habitats provides cover for grass snakes, adders, foxes and badgers. In the skies above is a great variety of birds including: peregrine falcon, raven, crow, willow warbler, chiffchaff, blackcap, skylark, meadow pipit, whitethroat and rock pipit. Drop your gaze to the grasses and you might spot some of the down's butterflies and moths, such as: small eggar, chalkhill blue, brown argus, grayling, dingy skipper, grizzled skipper and yellow shell.

Opposite The north slopes of Brean Down represent one of a variety of habitats found here

Clockwise from top: Blackcap; adder; whitethroat; peregrine falcon; chalkhill blue

On and around the down

As you explore the down you will move between habitats. Sometimes you will find yourself right on the boundary between these different worlds. Pause for a moment and see how much diversity there is around you.

The north–south divide

Along the southern slopes on the shallow soils grows the unique plant community of the white rock rose, Somerset hair grass and dwarf sedge. These plants grow in just a few locations in the world, and only grow together on the southern slopes of Brean Down. The deeper soils of the northern slope are partly covered by an invasive scrub of hawthorn, wild privet, bramble and bracken. However, amongst this grow cowslips, wood sage, campion, common ragwort and spotted orchid. Here there is a profusion of bluebells that flower late due to the northern aspect. Below the cliffs at the south-eastern end of the down this scrub has developed into a small wood with ash, field maple and stinking iris.

Clockwise from left:
Spotted orchid; white rock rose; stinking iris; dwarf sedge; common ragwort

Growing in the grasses

Along the top of the down the limestone grassland includes: horseshoe vetch, fescue grass, salad burnet, scabious, yellow wort, fairy flax, wild carrot, Goldilocks aster, sheep fescue and thyme. Along the coastal edge there are sea pink, sea campion, stagshorn plantain, brome and scurvy grass.

Clockwise from above:
Fairy flax; wild carrot; sea pink; salad burnet; sea campion

Clockwise from below:
Dunlin; wigeon; redshank; ringed plover

At the water's edge

The Severn Estuary is a Ramsar site, a wetland designated of international importance under the Ramsar Convention. It is a moulting ground for shelduck and dunlin, where adult birds shed their worn-out feathers from the year's breeding season and grow new, strong, warm feathers to see them through the winter. Wigeon also over-winter here. There are internationally important numbers of whimbrel and black-tailed godwit, as well as curlew, redshank, ringed plover, grey plover, common snipe and oystercatcher.

Almost an Island

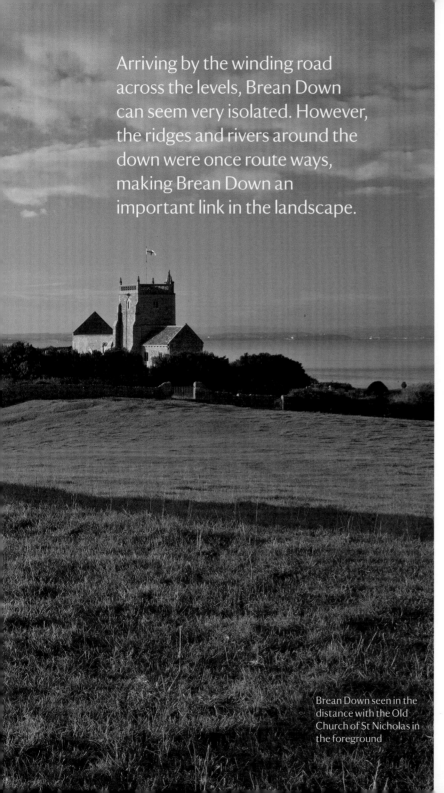

Arriving by the winding road across the levels, Brean Down can seem very isolated. However, the ridges and rivers around the down were once route ways, making Brean Down an important link in the landscape.

Brean Down seen in the distance with the Old Church of St Nicholas in the foreground

From the down many hills can be seen that have Iron Age hillforts on top of them, such as Brent Knoll (NT), Dolebury Warren (NT) and Worlebury. The last was attacked by the Romans and abandoned, unlike the hillfort on Brean Down. The Romans extracted vast amounts of lead from the Mendips, which they exported down the River Axe. The treacherous waters required the construction of navigational aids such as lighthouses and signal stations. Traces of a round Roman structure, which could be either, survive on Steep Holm. Stone for the Roman temple on Brean Down came from Bleadon Hill, the Polden Hills and the Bristol and Bath areas. Towards the end of the Roman period, temples were also built on hills such as Cadbury hillfort (NT) near Clevedon and Cadbury Camp hillfort near Congresbury.

Saints and shipwrecks

The hermit who moved onto the down may have come from Ireland or been inspired by early Irish missionaries. From the sixth century other Christian monks made their homes here, including St Gildas (later Abbot of Glastonbury Abbey) on Steep Holm, St Cadoc on Flat Holm and St Congar at Cadbury hillfort near Congresbury. The church at Uphill is clearly visible from Brean Down above the River Axe, its tower then painted white as a navigational aid.

The shape of the hills themselves was used for navigation. The distinctly shaped Crook Peak was ominously known as See-Me-Not. Evidence of the hazardousness of these waters can be seen south of the down. At low tide a dark V of stone can be seen. This is a fishweir used to guide fish towards a trap at the point of the V. Next to the fishweir the ribs of an unidentified wrecked wooden ship protrude from the mud. Another wreck of a 17th-century Portuguese ship lies by the tip of the down. There are probably many more wrecks buried beneath the mud.

The importance of Brean Down

Brean Down's prominence, visible from afar with the same far-reaching views in all directions, has meant it has always been of strategic importance. For hundreds of years, kings and generals have kept it in their line of defence.

The easy accessibility of this area by river could be dangerous, hence a Roman fleet being based at Cardiff. After the Romans left, there were raids along this coast. In one of them, the young St Patrick may have been abducted from Somerset and taken away to Ireland. Vikings built a temporary encampment on the end of the Polden Hills and made use of the holm islands. There is also a story that they sailed up the River Axe past Brean Down to raid the village of Bleadon. It is said that they were thwarted by the actions of a local woman: 'On Axe's quay, the vessels lay, the Danes their swords uplifting. A Bleadon wife brought forth a knife and sent them all a drifting.'

A local Celtic British army may have made their last stand at Brean Down, using the hillfort as a refuge, with the river behind intended as an escape route. They were unsuccessful, as the *Anglo-Saxon Chronicle* records in the year 614 that the King of the West Saxons and his son, Cynegils and Cwichelm, 'fought at Beandun, and slew two thousand and sixty-five Welsh.' This was part of the steady westward drive of Anglo-Saxon conquests of the area that turned the River Severn into a frontier.

Centuries in the making

In 1539 the defence of the River Severn was considered by King Henry VII, when he had the coast surveyed. Defensive fortifications called 'blockhouses' were proposed and possibly even started, one at Middle Hope (NT) by the

Above Viewed from Lavernock Point in Wales: wooded Worlebury Hill on the left, Flat Holm with its lighthouse before the high West Knoll of Brean Down, Brent Knoll and finally Steep Holm

mouth of the River Yeo, and two at Uphill presumably on either side of the river, with one sited on Brean Down. However, while we lack evidence for the blockhouses, beacons for warning fires were definitely built in the area.

A working defence had to wait until the late 19th century, when Brean Down became part of an important chain of forts that stretched across to Lavernock Point in Wales via the islands of Flat Holm and Steep Holm. Each island has the remains of forts similar to that at the end of Brean Down, but each with a design unique for their location and shape. This chain of forts was created to catch enemy ships in a deadly crossfire. They were in use from 1870–1900. The process was repeated again in the Second World War, only this time with more powerful guns. These defences were never put to the test, so how effective they would have been is hard to gauge.

Making contact

On 18 May 1897 a kite was flown from the top of the down and used as an aerial to send a signal to Lavernock Point. This was part of the demonstration of the world's first radio transmission across water. This wireless messaging equipment was set up by Guglielmo Marconi, who had invented the equipment just two years before. Marconi's first assistant, George Kemp, kept a diary during the Bristol Channel experiments, in which he made sketches recording this historic leap in telephony. The scientist Lord Kelvin witnessed this important event but he was not impressed: 'Telegraphy without wires is all very well, but I'd rather send a message by a boy on a pony!'

A changing environment

Time does not stand still on the down. It is always changing. Brean Down's exposed position surrounded by low-lying land makes it both attractive to visitors for its panoramic views, but also leaves it exposed to climatic conditions.

The thin soils make both the plants and archaeology vulnerable to any changes. During the foot and mouth outbreak, when the down was closed to visitors, the grazing cattle changed their regular routes. New soil was exposed and then heavy rain rapidly accelerated the process, creating a deep trench.

Visitors are naturally drawn to the top of the hills. Unfortunately, this means that the main route runs right across the top of the highest concentration of archaeological remains. This route even crosses the exposed remains of the Roman temple. However, any alternative route would only take the footfall across other equally vulnerable features such as the burial mounds.

Above The size of the Severn's tidal range has led to proposals to build a barrage across it to harness this natural energy

The threat of the sea

Storms and erosion can reveal archaeological evidence, but once exposed it has to be quickly saved before it is lost. One example is the Bronze Age burial, found when the beach was stripped of sand in a storm in 1936. Two beaker pots were found in a shallow hollow near the sand cliff. The Bronze Age settlement in the sand cliff was also discovered by artefacts eroding from the cliff. It was excavated and large protective boulders and gabions (stone-filled cages) installed.

The tidal mud to the south of the down is slowly eroding away, exposing the stone fishweir and the shipwreck next to it. Many of the buildings on the edges of the down are succumbing to the power of the sea, either being directly pounded by waves or slowly corroded by the salty sea spray.

A barrage too far?

As the climate changes, storms are becoming more frequent and the sea level is rising. One response to climate change is the often-proposed barrage across the River Severn, which would harness its vast tidal power to generate electricity. Early plans showed it using Brean Down and both of the holm islands as part of the structure. More recent proposals have it avoiding the islands and making landfall to the south of the down, protecting it from stormy seas, but carrying a large road near by.

Time and tide

Whatever our response to these environmental concerns, it is an accepted fact that the climate has changed and will continue to do so, changing the landscape in the process. Along the south side of the West Knoll are the down's most ancient archaeological features. Outlines of terraces and cliffs of ancient beaches mark former sea levels at 12–14 metres (40–47 feet), 21 metres (70 feet) and 36–43 metres (120–140 feet) above the current high-tide mark. In the very long term, the seas will make Brean Down an island once more, as it was long before the last Ice Age.

Below As the climate changes Brean Down will see more frequent and violent storms and extremes of weather

A 360° tour

There are fantastic views reaching for up to 42 miles (68 kilometres). The illustrated panoramas opposite give an 'ideal' view from Brean Down. What you can see will vary depending on where you stand on the down, and of course the prevailing weather, but nearly everything is visible from the trig point on the West Knoll.

To the west, out to sea, are the two islands of Steep Holm and Flat Holm, with the coast of Wales beyond. The city of Cardiff, including some of its landmarks, can be seen. If you have binoculars, you should be able to see Castle Coch. The red turrets of this 19th-century Gothic Revival castle rise up from amongst the trees above the city.

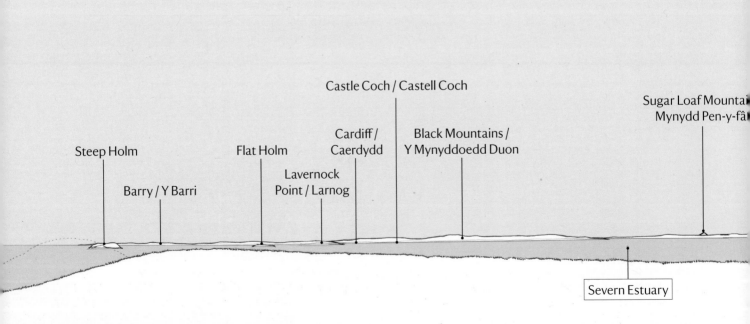

Castle Coch / Castell Coch

Sugar Loaf Mountai
Mynydd Pen-y-fâ

Cardiff /
Caerdydd

Black Mountains /
Y Mynyddoedd Duon

Steep Holm

Flat Holm

Lavernock
Point / Larnog

Barry / Y Barri

Severn Estuary